A New Pet

by Mary Lindeen

NORWOOD HOUSE PRESS

DEAR CAREGIVER, The *Beginning to Read—Read and Discover* books provide emergent readers the opportunity to explore the world through nonfiction while building early reading skills. The text integrates both common sight words and content vocabulary. These key words are featured on lists provided at the back of the book to help your child expand his or her sight word recognition, which helps build reading fluency. The content words expand vocabulary and support comprehension.

Nonfiction text is any text that is factual. The Common Core State Standards call for an increase in the amount of informational text reading among students. The Standards aim to promote college and career readiness among students. Preparation for college and career endeavors requires proficiency in reading complex informational texts in a variety of content areas. You can help your child build a foundation by introducing nonfiction early. To further support the CCSS, you will find Reading Reinforcement activities at the back of the book that are aligned to these Standards.

Above all, the most important part of the reading experience is to have fun and enjoy it!

Sincerely,

Shannon Cannon

Shannon Cannon, Ph.D.
Literacy Consultant

Norwood House Press
For more information about Norwood House Press please visit our website at www.norwoodhousepress.com or call 866-565-2900.
© 2022 Norwood House Press. Beginning-to-Read™ is a trademark of Norwood House Press. All rights reserved. No part of this book may be reproduced or utilized in any form or by any means without written permission from the publisher.

Editor: Judy Kentor Schmauss
Designer: Sara Radka

Photo Credits:
Getty Images, cover, 1, 4–28; Shutterstock, 3

Library of Congress Cataloging-in-Publication Data
Names: Lindeen, Mary, author.
Title: A new pet / by Mary Lindeen.
Description: Chicago : Norwood House Press, 2022. | Series: A beginning-to-read book | Audience: Grades
    K-1 | Summary: "Describes what it takes to care for a new pet, including what pets need and how to keep
    them safe and healthy. This title includes a note to caregivers, reading activities, and a word list. An early
    social and emotional book that includes reading activities and a word list"– Provided by publisher.
Identifiers: LCCN 2021049725 (print) | LCCN 2021049726 (ebook) | ISBN 9781684507870
    (hardcover) | ISBN 9781684047352 (paperback) | ISBN 9781684047390 (epub)
Subjects: LCSH: Pets–Juvenile literature.
Classification: LCC SF416.2 .L55 2022 (print) | LCC SF416.2 (ebook) | DDC 636.088/7–dc23/eng/20211108
LC record available at https://lccn.loc.gov/2021049725
LC ebook record available at https://lccn.loc.gov/2021049726

Hardcover ISBN: 978-1-68450-787-0
Paperback ISBN: 978-1-68404-735-2

This bed is for a new pet.

So are these bowls.

This new pet
is a dog!

This new pet is a guinea pig.

A guinea pig lives in a cage.

Guinea pigs
drink from
water bottles.

They eat from
small dishes.

This new pet is soft and smooth.

It's a gecko.

It has very sticky feet!

Geckos live in small tanks.

The tanks are warm and dry.

New pets come
in many shapes
and sizes.

But they all need
the same things.

They need a place to sleep.

Small pets need small spaces.

Big pets need big spaces.

They also need
the right kind
of food to eat.

New pets need water, too.

Some need a little bit of water.

Others need a lot!

Pets need to
exercise, too.

Every pet needs
to exercise
every day.

Most pets need
our help
to exercise.

New pets need our friendship, too.

They want to be with us a lot of the time.

But sometimes they want to be alone.

A new pet needs
many things—
including our love!

. . . READING REINFORCEMENT . . .

CRAFT AND STRUCTURE

To check your child's understanding of the organization of the book, recreate the following chart on a sheet of paper. Ask your child to complete the chart by writing different things a new pet needs:

VOCABULARY: Learning Content Words

Content words are words that are specific to a particular topic. All the content words in this book can be found on page 32. Use some or all of these content words to complete one or more of the following activities:

1. Have your child find word parts or smaller words within a word.

2. Help your child learn and practice new words by making word cards that have a word and a picture on each card.

3. Write two sets of the words on index cards. Lay them facedown and play Concentration with your child.

4. Take turns with your child acting out and guessing the words.

5. Tell your child a word and have them define it and use it in a sentence.

FOUNDATIONAL SKILLS: Long Vowel Sounds

The sound made by a long vowel is the same as its name: *a, e, i, o, u*. Have your child identify words with long vowels in the list below. Then help your child find words with long vowels in this book.

spike   wrote   cube

clock   dump   trade

CLOSE READING OF INFORMATIONAL TEXT

Close reading helps children comprehend text. It includes reading a text, discussing it with others, and answering questions about it. Use these questions to discuss this book with your child:

1. How are a guinea pig, a rabbit, and a mouse similar?
2. What might happen if you gave your pet the wrong kind of food?
3. How are pets and humans similar?
4. Why do you think pets need to be around people?
5. What does it mean to "take care of" something?
6. What kind of pet would you like to have? Why?

FLUENCY

Fluency is the ability to read accurately with speed and expression. Help your child practice fluency by using one or more of the following activities:

1. Reread the book to your child at least two times while he or she uses a finger to track each word as it is read.
2. Read a line of the book, then reread it as your child reads along with you.
3. Ask your child to go back through the book and read the words he or she knows.
4. Have your child practice reading the book several times to improve accuracy, rate, and expression.

··· Word List ···

A New Pet uses the 79 words listed below. *High-frequency words* are those words that are used most often in the English language. They are sometimes referred to as *sight words* because children need to learn to recognize them automatically when they read. *Content words* are any words specific to a particular topic. Regular practice reading these words will enhance your child's ability to read with greater fluency and comprehension.

High-Frequency Words

a	day	it	right	this
all	eat	little	same	time
also	every	many	small	to
and	for	most	so	too
are	from	new	some	us
be	has	of	the	very
big	help	other(s)	these	want
but	in	our	they	water
come	is	place	things	with

Content Words

alone	dog	gecko(s)	love	soft
bed	drink	guinea pig(s)	need(s)	sometimes
bit	dry	including	pet(s)	spaces
bottles	exercise	it's	shapes	sticky
bowls	feet	kind	sizes	tanks
cage	food	live(s)	sleep	warm
dishes	friendship	lot	smooth	

··· About the Author

Mary Lindeen is a writer, editor, parent, and former elementary school teacher. She has written more than 100 books for children and edited many more. She specializes in early literacy instruction and books for young readers, especially nonfiction.